SIT & SOLVE

Lickety Split Crosswords

Doug Peterson

PUZZLE
WRIGHT
PRESS

New York

PUZZLEWRIGHT PRESS, the distinctive Puzzlewright Press logo, and Sit & Solve
are registered trademarks of Sterling Publishing Co., Inc.

© 2014 by Doug Peterson
Published by Sterling Publishing Co., Inc.
387 Park Avenue South, New York, NY 10016

ISBN 978-1-4549-1166-1

Distributed in Canada by Sterling Publishing
c/o Canadian Manda Group, 165 Dufferin Street
Toronto, Ontario, Canada M6K 3H6
Distributed in the United Kingdom by GMC Distribution Services
Castle Place, 166 High Street, Lewes, East Sussex, England BN7 1XU
Distributed in Australia by Capricorn Link (Australia) Pty. Ltd.
P.O. Box 704, Windsor, NSW 2756, Australia

For information about custom editions, special sales, and premium and corporate purchases,
please contact Sterling Special Sales at 800-805-5489 or specialsales@sterlingpublishing.com.

Manufactured in China

2   4   6   8   10   9   7   5   3   1

www.puzzlewright.com

Contents

Introduction

When Halloween season rolls around, I like to buy a few bags of "Fun Size" candy bars. They're smaller versions of all your favorite chocolaty treats, just the right size for the little trick-or-treaters. And they're "fun" because you can get away with eating four or five candy bars in one sitting and not feel guilty about it!

I think "Fun Size" is also a great way to describe the puzzles in this book. They're smaller than the puzzles you'll find in your daily paper and jam-packed with fun entries and clever clues. And each puzzle contains a mini-theme, meaning the two longest answers in each grid are related somehow. Some of the themes are straightforward. Some are more subtle. And they're all fun. Perfect for solving while you munch on a chocolate bar or two.

Many thanks to Angela "PuzzleGirl" Halsted, test-solver extraordinaire.
—Doug Peterson

6

ACROSS
1 Nut used in pies
6 Traffic snarls
10 Skiing locale
11 Skinned knee, in kidspeak
12 Handheld device that runs apps
14 Canine visitor to Oz
15 Perfectly pitched, musically
16 Super Bowl org.
18 Period in history
19 One of Santa's helpers
22 "Malcolm X" director Spike
24 Brother of Huey and Dewey
26 Bill killer
30 Small freight elevator
32 Fencing sword
33 Cable movie channel
34 "Give it a ___!"
35 Place for a barbecue

DOWN
1 "Hey, over here!"
2 "Sesame Street" favorite
3 Nail polish layer
4 Chef's garment
5 Volleyball barrier
6 President Adams or Kennedy
7 Stopped snoozing
8 Worker with a pick
9 "I'm outta here!"
13 ___ vault
17 Traveled in a jet

19 Revered figure
20 Jeweler's magnifying glass
21 Vapors
23 "Don't Cry for Me, Argentina" musical
25 "Yeah, right!"
27 Coup d'___
28 Hatcher of "Desperate Housewives"
29 Rice-shaped pasta
31 Snake that killed Cleopatra

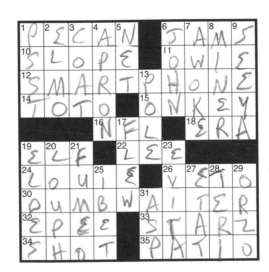

8

ACROSS

1 Smashes into
5 Tibetan priests
10 Perched on
11 Not approximate
12 Back of the neck
13 Tin Pan ___
14 Saints quarterback who was the MVP of Super Bowl XLIV
16 Tries for, at an auction
17 Technique
22 Vodka cocktail with cranberry and grapefruit juice
25 Old name for Myanmar
26 Mess maker
27 Radar images
28 Stuff in a dryer trap
29 Adventure for a knight
30 Kindling choppers

DOWN

1 Ray Charles's genre, briefly
2 Pong company
3 Fuel-efficient two-wheeler
4 Gushes
5 Successful student
6 Bar between wheels
7 Like a peacock
8 Flexible blackjack cards
9 Pigpen
15 Pompous talk
18 Inventor Nikola
19 Double ___ (DNA shape)

20 Atmospheric layer
21 Borrower's burdens
22 George Takei's "Star Trek" role
23 First Great Lake, alphabetically
24 Guitar boosters
25 Fourth of July party, for short

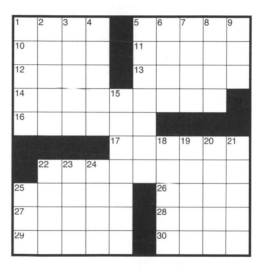

ACROSS

1 Ham, lamb, or Spam
5 Buddy of "The Beverly Hillbillies"
10 Pita-wrapped sandwich
11 Instant replay technique
12 Superman's home
14 State north of Wyoming
15 Use a broom
18 "Snow White" frame
19 Singer/actress Zadora
20 Krispy ___ Doughnuts
22 Chic
25 Batman's home
29 Midnight follower
30 Neighborhood
31 Fruit-filled desserts
32 Pikes ___ (Colorado landmark)

DOWN

1 "The Wizard of Oz" studio
2 Hand-___ coordination
3 Gallery hangings
4 Singer nicknamed "The Velvet Fog"
5 "Baseball Tonight" channel
6 Ink stain
7 Comfort
8 "Lose Yourself" rapper
9 Cash register key

13 "Alley ___"
15 Faucet
16 Ryder of
   Hollywood
17 Spring holiday
20 Airline to
   Amsterdam
21 News summary
23 Not this
24 Thanksgiving side
   dish
26 Indignation
27 Lipton product
28 Chatter on and on

ACROSS

1 Mustangs, e.g.
6 Inning enders
10 WWII German sub
11 "That was a close one!"
12 Outdoor space for community gatherings
14 Piquancy
15 Seize by force
16 Greek vowel
18 Ignited
19 Horror director Craven

22 Sailor's "Yes!"
24 Info from spies, briefly
26 "Swan ___"
30 Mysterious pattern in a cornfield, say
32 Military takeover
33 "Psycho" setting
34 Prey for aardvarks
35 Kvetcher's phrase

DOWN

1 Fiddle (with)
2 Slender instrument

3 Spreadsheet lines
4 "Divine Comedy" poet
5 Ave. crossers
6 Numbered composition
7 Big name in rental trucks
8 Country singer Clark or Gibbs
9 Cleaned out, as a chimney
13 Wharf
17 Soft rock?
19 Coven member's religion, perhaps

20 Infamous energy company
21 Heavily built
23 George Jetson's boy
25 Actor Omar of "House"
27 End of "Hamlet" or "Macbeth"
28 Swiss painter Paul
29 Slippery
31 "As I see it," in an e-mail

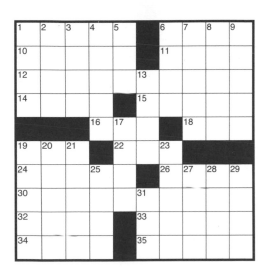

ACROSS

1 Job to do
5 Shredded ___
10 "Garfield" pooch
11 Energetic
12 Of low quality
13 Scrooge, for one
14 Dried plum
16 Birdbrain
17 "___ and the City"
18 Not at all cheerful
20 Sheet of floating ice
22 ___ Pérignon (pricey champagne)

25 Two-part
27 Unmanned aircraft
29 Muhammad Ali's faith
31 Flabbergasts
32 "Scooby-Doo" girl in a turtleneck and glasses
33 Antelopes of the Serengeti
34 English class assignment
35 Cable TV sports award

DOWN

1 Big baseball card brand
2 Love to pieces
3 Largest city in the Dakotas
4 "Ol' Man River" composer Jerome
5 Typist's speed measure: Abbr.
6 Klum of "Project Runway"
7 English racecourse with an annual Derby

8 Did an imitation of

9 Newbie

15 It may need a boost

19 Color of Superman's cape

21 Wool-bearing beast

23 Get the better of

24 Unkempt

25 Sleazy bar

26 Puts into action

28 Go ballistic

30 Fifth calendar page

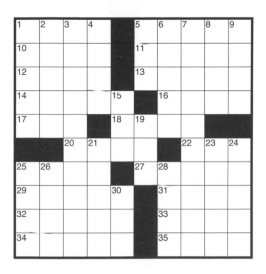

ACROSS

1 Tomato variety
5 French pancake
10 Bad to the bone
11 Jeopardy
12 Arm-twisting wrestling hold
14 First-stringers
15 Gives a "Jeopardy!" response
16 Dream world?
17 To the ___ (completely)
19 Place with spinning classes
20 Chum
23 Start of a play
26 Plumber in many video games
28 Manicurist's application
30 Squiggly mark in "jalapeño"
31 Bartók or Lugosi
32 Spouse's mom, for one
33 Arabian Sea gulf

DOWN

1 Post-injury program
2 Egg-shaped
3 Played charades
4 ___ mater
5 Life-saving skill practiced on dummies
6 Kick back
7 Cupid, to the Greeks
8 Choose
9 Fraternal group
13 Award for a sitcom star
18 BBs and bullets
19 Original "SNL" cast member Radner

20 Was too inquisitive
21 Airplane divider
22 Lindsay of "Mean Girls"
23 Not for
24 Brother of Abel
25 Cash register drawer
27 "Sin City" actress Jessica
29 Bench for believers

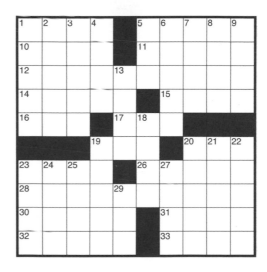

ACROSS
1 All-inclusive
5 "Back in ___" (AC/DC album)
10 Lacking in tact
11 Dangerous gas
12 Toddler's beddy-bye spot
13 Nostalgic tune
14 Rex Stout's orchid-loving detective
16 Raggedy ___
17 Mountain road's shape
18 "Eureka!"
21 Tombstone letters
23 "Your Show of Shows" star
27 Tempest
28 Polite interruption
30 Energize, informally
31 Take it on the chin
32 Doles (out)
33 Urban legend

DOWN
1 Eyebrow shape
2 Change direction
3 Drooling dog in the funny pages
4 Black-and-white zoo attraction
5 Square chocolate treat
6 Composer Schifrin
7 Discombobulate
8 Hairdos
9 Miniskirts reveal them
15 Freeway entrances
18 Tea-producing region of India

19 Blackjack request
20 Start a family, perhaps
22 Sacred song
24 Rock's Mötley ___
25 "Yo, sailor!"
26 Take a breather
29 Sound that means "I'm not impressed"

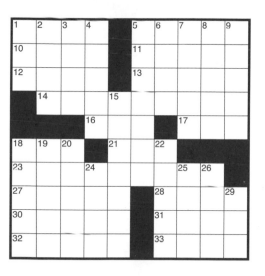

ACROSS

1 Novelist Cather
6 Rubs the wrong way
10 Manner of speaking
11 Sony laptop brand
12 Hawaiian island
13 "___ my dead body!"
14 Portable computer storage device
16 Palindromic distress signal
17 Place, as a bet
18 Aye, in Versailles
19 Org. that publishes Shooting Illustrated
22 Chicken wings, ribs, etc.
26 Got more mature
27 Volunteer's offer
28 Arrive
29 Thoroughly enjoy
30 1982 Disney sci-fi flick
31 Like cotton candy

DOWN

1 Goes limp
2 Neighbor of Oregon
3 Little brother of Lucy
4 Rich soil
5 Ethel Waters hit of 1929
6 Tusk material
7 Sitar player Shankar
8 Ukraine's capital
9 Ticked off

15 Milk and cheese suppliers
18 City in northern Utah
19 Actor Nick of "Affliction"
20 Scoundrel
21 Take in, as a stray dog
22 "Is that a ___?"
23 Stereotypical lab assistant
24 Lost clownfish of film
25 Defect

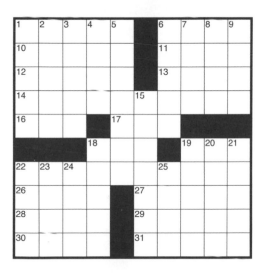

ACROSS
1 Bad thing to bounce
6 Startled reaction
10 Capital of Vietnam
11 Stench
12 Verb on a campaign poster
13 Connect Four, e.g.
14 Patron saint of sailors
15 "Wizards of Waverly Place" star Selena

16 Hotel room door opener
18 Hamlet's trusted friend
22 "Wheel of Fortune" host Pat
25 Have a snack
26 Small songbird
27 Central Florida city
28 Classroom assistant
29 ___ Rapids, Iowa
30 It gets hammered
31 "I'll help if I can!"

DOWN
1 Place for blush
2 Tinseltown's Berry
3 Foe
4 "No. 5" fragrance creator
5 Hobby shop purchase
6 '60s disco entertainer in a cage
7 Eve's mate
8 A few
9 Informal D.C. title

15 Watchdog's warning
17 Thumbs-up response
19 Sycophant
20 Its believers worship Allah
21 Windy City airport
22 "Black ___" (2010 Natalie Portman film)
23 Operatic highlight
24 "Star Wars" knight
27 Autumn mo.

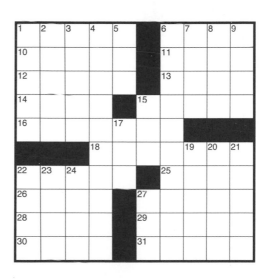

ACROSS

1 Astronaut Grissom
4 From Florence, e.g.
10 Santa ___ winds
11 "Dr. No" Bond girl Andress
12 Airport-to-hotel vehicle
14 ___ noir (red wine)
15 Physicians' gp.
16 Pancake flipper
19 Speak hesitantly
23 Curtain holder
26 Dinero
27 Enthusiastic amateur photographer
30 Eyesight
31 Wedding vow
32 Powerfully effective
33 Thriller novelist Deighton

DOWN

1 Struggles to breathe
2 Not cool
3 Steam room
4 Finger-wagger's words
5 Address at the top of a browser
6 NNW's opposite
7 Island south of Florida
8 School reunion attendee
9 Kennedy Space Center org.
13 Preschool attendees
17 Weep for
18 Love, to a Latino

20 Exxon merger partner
21 Slip away from
22 Make fun of
23 Abbr. on an invitation
24 Kent State's state
25 Check for fingerprints
28 Reason for overtime
29 "This weighs a ___!"

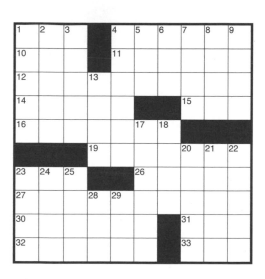

ACROSS

1 Interior design
6 Band worn at a beauty pageant
10 Waikiki welcome
11 "___ the Woods" (Sondheim musical)
12 Young wedding party member
14 Spell checker's find
15 Objectors
16 Shake, as one's tail
18 Suited to the task
19 TV drama set in Vegas
22 Evil spell
24 Sleep malady
26 Musical McEntire
30 Young wedding party member
32 Ship's prison
33 Legendary lawman Earp
34 Visualizes
35 Piece in The New Yorker

DOWN

1 Off one's rocker
2 TV hillbilly ___ May Clampett
3 Henhouse
4 "Unbelievable!"
5 Actress ___ Dawn Chong
6 Horoscope heading
7 Santa ___ Park (California racetrack)
8 Prepare to bathe
9 "The Planets" composer Gustav
13 Fit of anger
17 Captain who pursues Moby Dick
19 Atkins Diet no-nos

20 Tapering topper
21 Belly button type
23 Body shots?
25 Refrigerator door items
27 Notable times
28 Letter after alpha
29 Bohemian
31 She has little lambs

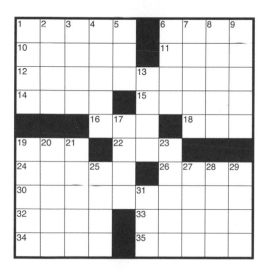

ACROSS

1 Cambodia's continent
5 ___ legend ("MythBusters" target)
10 Explorer Juan Ponce de ___
11 Cuddly-looking marsupial
12 Guessing game with hits and misses
14 Flabbergast
15 Comfort
16 Stops in to see
18 Original "Charlie's Angels" actress Smith
22 Lotion ingredient
23 Longtime Cuban leader Castro
28 Guessing game for amateur artists
30 Kindle download
31 Goatee's place
32 Keaton or Lane
33 Answer man Trebek

DOWN

1 Jessica of "Fantastic Four"
2 Clothes line?
3 Minuscule amount
4 1998 animated film about an insect colony
5 Luau guitar, for short
6 "___ are red ..."
7 Religion founded in Persia
8 Elite group of celebs
9 Neck areas

13 Impose, as a tax
17 Data, briefly
18 Poked fun at
19 Courtroom excuse
20 Drink with marshmallows
21 Divulge
24 Ancient Peruvian
25 Willy Wonka creator Roald
26 Toledo's lake
27 Medium-sized wildcat
29 President between Harry and Jack

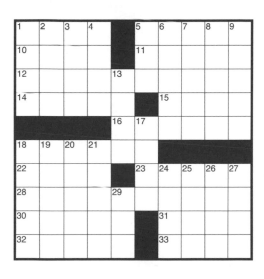

ACROSS

1 Actress Blanchett
5 Earring holders
10 Chopped down
11 Hank with 755 homers
12 Dry as a bone
13 Hefty horned beast
14 Hairstyle associated with Audrey Hepburn
16 Avoid a trial
17 Enter with an army

22 Powdered candy in a strawlike wrapper
24 Fictional girl of the Swiss Alps
26 "Winning ___ everything"
27 Honey-colored
28 Will who played Grandpa Walton
29 Hefty horns
30 Zilch

DOWN

1 Blokes
2 Condor's home

3 Between, in poetry
4 Call off the romance
5 "Grand" crime
6 Honolulu's home
7 Englishman, informally
8 Long, long time
9 ___-cone
15 Magic potions
18 Two-finger gesture
19 In unfamiliar territory
20 Enjoyed a meal

21 Crowd scene actor
22 ___ Zero (Diet Dr Pepper rival)
23 "What's the big ___?"
24 Fedora, e.g.
25 Ostrich relative

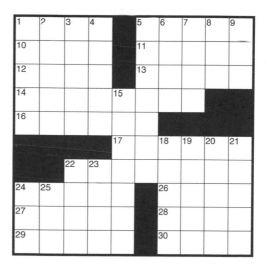

ACROSS

1 Protractor's measure
6 Island nation west of Tonga
10 German sausage
11 Colored part of the eye
12 Star of "The Wonder Years"
14 Take advantage of
15 Tightly packed
16 Camera protector
19 Spot for an afternoon nap
23 For the birds?
26 Rap's Dr. ___
27 Bassist for the Sex Pistols
30 Arthroscopic surgery site
31 Make smile
32 Burn slightly
33 Middle age, roughly

DOWN

1 Worse than bad
2 Hospital staffer
3 "___ Acres" ('60s sitcom)
4 '60s psychedelic
5 UFO crew, perhaps
6 Quitting time, for many
7 Tehran's land
8 Lively dances
9 "Much clearer!"
13 Sandler of "The Wedding Singer"
17 Electric razor
18 "How ___ refuse?"
20 Scent, in Sheffield
21 Pizza's outer edge

22 "One Flew Over the Cuckoo's Nest" author
23 Makes inquiries
24 Grape holder
25 Creative thought
28 Half-___ (Starbucks order)
29 Text messager's "I think ..."

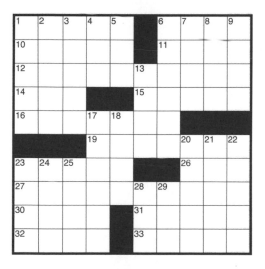

ACROSS

1 Clumps of grass
6 Boot's bottom
10 Turn the other ___
11 All fired up
12 Deputy on "The Andy Griffith Show"
14 "Tasty!"
15 Dull gray in color
16 One-dimensional
18 Moral principles
21 Route for ships
24 Chicken ___ king
26 Large bowl-shaped musical instrument
28 "What's gotten ___ you?"
29 Love to pieces
30 Actress Cannon
31 Lends a hand

DOWN

1 Frozen dessert chain
2 Moving day rental
3 Manhattan Project physicist Enrico
4 Lowest card in a royal flush
5 Bony
6 Jungle adventure
7 "Metamorphoses" poet
8 Board game or cereal
9 "East of ___"
13 "All right, all right, I get it!"
17 Isaac or Wayne

19 Mom on "The Brady Bunch"
20 Drink indelicately
21 Lose traction
22 Start of a counting rhyme
23 Start of an encouraging cry
25 City north of Des Moines
27 JFK's predecessor

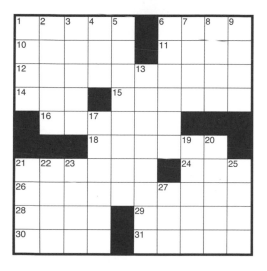

ACROSS

1 Blue toon
6 Wife of Zeus
10 Divided Asian country
11 Swedish actress Lena
12 Part of the psyche to "get in touch with"
14 Tree trunk growth
15 Deschanel of "New Girl"
16 Org. concerned with clean air
18 Six-pt. scores
19 Butter portion
22 Clickable address
24 More hazardous, as a winter sidewalk
26 Melodramatic "Rats!"
30 "Star Trek" setting
32 Russia's ___ Mountains
33 Historic English county
34 Without
35 Overgrown with dandelions, say

DOWN

1 ___ milk
2 "The kissing disease"
3 Beverage dispensers
4 Witherspoon of "Walk the Line"
5 At a distance
6 Syllables from Santa
7 Poet who inspired "Cats"
8 Hot under the collar
9 Raggedy dolls

13 Captain of
   industry
17 Contented
   murmur
19 God-fearing
20 TSX automaker
21 Tennessee NFLer
23 Moment of
   forgetfulness
25 Slender swimmers
27 Use a surgical
   beam
28 Scored 100% on
29 Alluring
31 Do some stitching

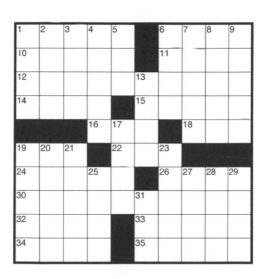

ACROSS

1 "___ to Be Wild"
5 "Stand and Deliver" Oscar nominee
10 Follow orders
11 Humdinger
12 Basis for "Man of La Mancha"
14 1988 Olympics city
15 Numbered hwy.
16 Monogram letter
19 Proclaim
22 Chat room "I believe"
23 Spot for a ball and chain
27 Chain that sells Blizzards
30 Mount climbed by Moses
31 Enjoy a novel
32 Mary-Kate or Ashley
33 Antlered animals

DOWN

1 Physiques, casually
2 Clarinet cousin
3 City with slots
4 Before-bedtime cold medicine
5 ___-Wan Kenobi
6 Comic book villain Luthor
7 Native New Zealander
8 "I'm ___ here!"
9 Broadsword material
13 Wrist-to-elbow bone
17 Persian Gulf country
18 Professor's goal

19 Reply to a childish taunt

20 Spammer's medium

21 Silver dollars, e.g.

24 On an even ___

25 Security breach

26 Terminates

28 "Norma ___" (Sally Field film)

29 Yang's counterpart

ACROSS

1 Empty spaces
5 Capital of Ghana
10 Openly admit
11 Harder to come by
12 Starchy staple food from the South Pacific
14 Dance under a pole
15 ___ and ends
16 Golfer Ernie
17 Fruity spread
19 Michelle, to Malia and Sasha
20 "So that's it!"
23 One of the woodwinds
26 Like Cheerios
28 Legume used in succotash
30 Computer chip maker
31 Stone Age shelter
32 Long-legged bird
33 River of Hades

DOWN

1 Clark of "Gone With the Wind"
2 "Complicated" singer Lavigne
3 Limericks, e.g.
4 Cosmetics applicator
5 Dog pound sound
6 Ricochet
7 Yucky stuff
8 Senator Harry or actress Tara
9 Cultural pursuits
13 Martial arts school
18 Son of Venus
19 Coin collector?
20 Persistently bothered
21 Opposite of light
22 Building addition

23 Kimono sashes
24 Sacrifice ___
(baseball play)
25 Conductor
Klemperer
27 "Sesame Street"
subject
29 Moose relative

ACROSS

1 Good buddies
5 "Blue Ribbon" beer brand
10 Help with a heist
11 TV's "Kate & ___"
12 Frat party outfit
13 Rudely awaken
14 "House" star
16 Hair arrangements
17 Main arteries
22 "M" star
26 Giant squid's home
27 Desperate
28 Lose the goatee, say
29 Walkman successor
30 Cheated, in slang
31 Huey Lewis and the ___

DOWN

1 Maze options
2 "It's ___ time!"
3 Like most runway models
4 Lesley of "60 Minutes"
5 Umbrella for a sunny day
6 Baseball's Felipe or Moises
7 Become fuzzy
8 "Certainly, señor!"
9 Nantes noggin
15 Committed to memory
18 "The Thinker" sculptor
19 Utter nonsense
20 "One way" indicator

21 Watermelon discards
22 Swank
23 Off-the-wall answer?
24 Drinks from bags
25 Gutter location

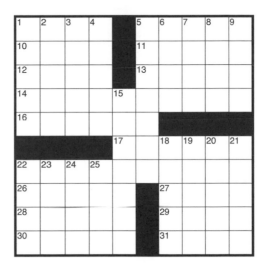

ACROSS

1 Stray from the script
6 On the same ___ (in sync)
10 Fragrant spring flower
11 "Such a pity!"
12 Highest rank for a young troop member
14 ___ gin fizz
15 Piano practice piece
16 Cowpoke's nickname
18 Easter egg coloring
19 Parsons of "The Big Bang Theory"
22 Sailor's assent
24 Amherst campus, familiarly
26 Change course abruptly
30 One of many earned by a 12-Across
32 Aspirin target
33 Rating a 10
34 Glitch
35 Flexible, like some straws

DOWN

1 Zoo attractions
2 "Let's Make a ___"
3 Nike's swoosh, for one
4 Narrow passage
5 "Later!"
6 Formal agreement
7 For all to hear
8 Flashy
9 Lauder of lipstick

44

13 Seductively attractive

17 Sunrise direction

19 Some checkers moves

20 "That is to say ..."

21 Tennis star Sharapova

23 Give the slip to

25 Do a number

27 Shangri-la

28 Quaint interjection

29 Depend (on)

31 Baby's chest protector

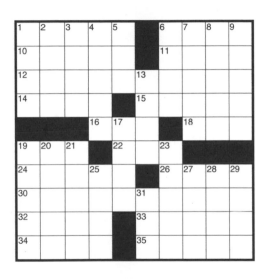

ACROSS

1 "Grand Hotel" star Greta
6 "Verb" or "adjective," e.g.
10 Lysol targets
11 Cosmonaut Gagarin
12 Gum in a green wrapper
14 Gerund suffix
15 Comics caveman Alley
16 Opinion
18 Title ogre in a 2001 film

22 Useful quality
24 Han ___ of "Star Wars"
25 Showgirl's scarf
27 "Barney & Friends" watcher
28 Gum in a yellow wrapper
32 Gumbo vegetable
33 Dishwasher cycle
34 Swarm
35 More peculiar

DOWN

1 Legendary naked horsewoman

2 Handsome hunk
3 Cheek reddeners
4 "Stepping away for a sec," in instant messages
5 Capital on a fjord
6 Divine maidens
7 "Absolutely," in Avignon
8 "Ode on a Grecian ___"
9 Tiny criticism
13 Canon camera line
17 Skype user's device
19 Plump

20 Fictional Plaza Hotel girl

21 "Welcome Back, ___" ('70s TV show starring Gabe Kaplan)

23 Easy-Bake Oven, e.g.

26 Hendrix hairdo

28 Write quickly

29 Island instrument, informally

30 Hot flash?

31 Get ___ of (toss out)

ACROSS

1 Carbonated
6 Letters on a radio switch
10 French farewell
11 Lioness in "The Lion King"
12 Party pooper
14 Hair removal brand
15 Honking flock
16 1860s White House nickname
18 Like a shrinking violet
19 Pitch caller
22 Trojans' sch.
24 Feds who make busts
26 Poems of devotion
30 Hodgepodge
32 Opera set in Egypt
33 ___-Seltzer
34 Not up to snuff
35 Blade sharpener

DOWN

1 Doe boy?
2 Brainchild
3 Tube-shaped pasta
4 Striped zoo attraction
5 Oscar winner Brynner
6 Diarist ___ Frank
7 Fabricates
8 ___ wound (superficial cut)
9 Brit's buddy
13 Many moons
17 ___ as a beaver
19 Open, as a flask
20 Hockey great Lemieux

21 Madrid museum
23 Place to play
   racquetball
25 Industry VIP
27 "New Look"
   designer Christian
28 Red Muppet
29 "Cut it out!"
31 NFL signal-callers

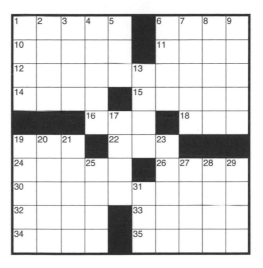

ACROSS
1 Muscle twitch
6 Lose your cool?
10 Supreme Court Justice Samuel
11 Designer Wang
12 "Bless you!" alternative
14 Mineo of moviedom
15 Having a talent for
16 Gets the mist off
18 Lousy
21 St. Francis of ___

24 Top number on some clock faces
26 Child prodigy
28 "On the Waterfront" director Kazan
29 Artist's stand
30 Binding obligation
31 Scatterbrained

DOWN
1 Hangs loosely
2 Beg
3 Path to the altar

4 Early Beatle Sutcliffe
5 Rikki-Tikki-Tavi, for one
6 Sajak or Seacrest, e.g.
7 Listen to
8 Pavarotti selection
9 Unit of power
13 Totally exhausted
17 Part of TGIF
19 Have a life
20 Dressed to the ___

21 Thunderstruck
22 One of Kirk's
   crewmen
23 Grumpy mood
25 In an aimless
   fashion
27 Chiang ___-shek

ACROSS

1 Soft drink in a red, white, and blue can
6 Strait-laced
10 Unrehearsed comment
11 Former "Tonight Show" host Jay
12 Suit material
13 Word processor command
14 Plaything for young builders
16 Tattoos, in slang
17 Wine and dine
18 Triangular sail
19 Biblical beast
22 Plaything for young builders
26 Drive, reverse, or neutral
27 Cringe in fear
28 Donated
29 City near Kyoto
30 Eject, as lava
31 Member of the violet family

DOWN

1 Singer Page or LaBelle
2 Buzz Aldrin's first name
3 Sharp, metallic sound
4 Fancy pajama material
5 "My bad!"
6 Ninth planet, until its 2006 demotion
7 Clinton cabinet member Janet
8 500-mile race, familiarly
9 Roundup sounds
15 1987 sci-fi film remade in 2014

18 L.L. Bean competitor
19 Dam on the Nile
20 Looks for
21 Dogcatcher's pickup
22 Quiche ingredients
23 Bring in, as crops
24 Christmas lights location
25 Historic Parks

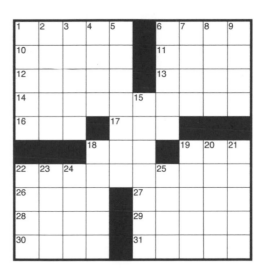

ACROSS
1 "Take a Chance on Me" band
5 Grammy winner Ronstadt
10 Pekoe and oolong
11 French ___ soup
12 Prohibition-era concoction
14 Bordeaux bye-bye
15 "This looks bad!"
16 Sound of disapproval
17 Extreme sport on two-wheelers
19 Cove

20 Middle "Brady Bunch" sister
23 Open a little
26 Limerick starter, often
28 Party for an expectant mom
30 Draw out
31 Remain unsettled
32 Surgical glove material
33 Bump off

DOWN
1 Facing the pitcher
2 Rosary units

3 Cloth-dyeing technique
4 Tennis legend Arthur
5 Reed or Rawls of music
6 Where e-mails show up
7 Close by, in poetry
8 "Nothin' ___!" ("Forget it!")
9 Part of A.D.
13 Instrument in a brass quintet
18 Tale of the Greek gods, e.g.

19 Utah's ___ Canyon National Park
20 Tiara twinkler
21 Sports facility
22 Dweebish
23 Brother of Cain
24 Actress Pinkett Smith
25 Share a border with
27 Ground ball bounces
29 "Facts of life" subject

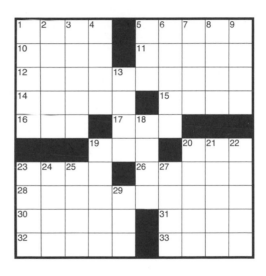

ACROSS
1 Badge of battle
5 Wrens and hens
10 Subtle glow
11 "David Copperfield" character Heep
12 Onion covering
13 ___ journalism (Hunter S. Thompson genre)
14 Fan of Metallica or Black Sabbath, say
16 Fella
17 Lofty poem
18 Type of tide
21 Yankee legend Gehrig
23 Shoe store whose employees wear striped shirts
28 Brightened
29 First word of "The Raven"
30 In unison
31 Vintage soda pop
32 Fort Worth resident
33 Glowing gas

DOWN
1 Girl Scout uniform accessory
2 Salad bar veggie
3 Diva's big song
4 Grammy category
5 Object of fear
6 "___ Man" (2008 superhero film)
7 Bandmate of John, Paul, and George
8 In a fog
9 Water's edge
15 Where relief pitchers warm up

18 D sharp's equivalent
19 State capital in the Northwest
20 Antiwrinkle treatment
22 The NCAA's Huskies
24 Fish in a can
25 "... with my banjo on my ___"
26 Canyon comeback
27 Horse rider's strap

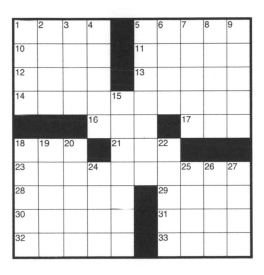

ACROSS

1 Tree seen in Southern California
5 Spills the beans
10 Stadium level
11 Get in the cross hairs
12 Hawaii's nickname
14 Shaggy Himalayan beast
15 Chicago Bulls' org.
16 Carne ___ (burrito filling)
19 Fan club's focus
20 Tug-of-war need
21 Yearly celebrations, for short
22 ___-Magnon
23 12-Across neckwear
24 1969 Barbra Streisand musical film
29 Small spot of land
30 Breezy sign-off
31 Preppy jackets
32 Much-maligned foreign car of the '80s

DOWN

1 ___ meeting
2 Feel rotten
3 Novelist Tolstoy
4 Dr. Jekyll's other half
5 Soak up the sun
6 Ignited
7 Actress Seyfried of "Les Misérables"
8 Kid in a dugout
9 Incredible bargains
13 Small battery size
16 Date for Betty or Veronica

17 Achy to the max
18 Moon-landing program
19 Utter foolishness
21 Fourposter, e.g.
23 Oodles
25 "Sweeney Todd" star Cariou
26 Lucy of "Ally McBeal"
27 Jet ___ (traveler's woe)
28 "___-hoo!"

ACROSS

1 Playwright Chekhov
6 Numbered instruction
10 Hardly hip
11 Heavenly circle
12 Where the Marx Brothers got their start
14 "For what ___ worth ..."
15 Late bedtime
16 Comes unglued
19 "Like a Virgin" was her first #1 single
23 Arrestee's excuse
26 Bubble filler
27 YouTube sensation
30 Sharif or Vizquel
31 Athletic shoe brand
32 Bookworm, in slang
33 Half-dozen half

DOWN

1 Blacksmith's block
2 "Spiffy!"
3 Bind tightly
4 Out of the ordinary
5 "Science Guy" Bill
6 Japanese religion
7 Word after folk or fairy
8 Fitzgerald of jazz
9 Wordsworth work
13 Nullify
17 Board a ship
18 Travel by ship
20 Low point
21 Brother's daughter
22 Popped up
23 Declare

24 Long motorcade vehicle
25 Country on the Caspian Sea
28 Big wine container
29 Suffix that means "kind of"

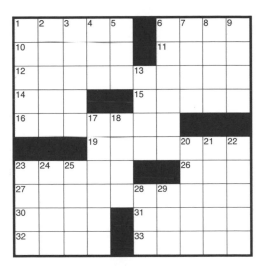

ACROSS

1 Labor leader Chavez
6 Q-tip, e.g.
10 "Wanted: Dead or ___"
11 Rocket-launching org.
12 Hot under the collar
13 Post-workout feeling
14 D.C. insider
15 Employee
17 Porker's pen
18 Dark and murky
19 Window insert
21 Laura's sitcom hubby
24 Apple music service
26 Lummox
27 "Round and Round" rock band
28 Unspoken
30 "Macbeth" has five
31 Deal maker
32 Vodka in a blue bottle
33 Football great Grier

DOWN

1 Moans and groans
2 Ness of "The Untouchables"
3 Bouncy toy sold in plastic eggs
4 Street sign abbr.
5 Chianti or claret
6 Sarcastic comments, slangily
7 '60s–'70s cartoon featuring Penelope Pitstop
8 Arthur ___ Stadium

9 Max Jr. of "The Beverly Hillbillies"

16 Lousy movie rating

20 Unable to sit still

22 Voice a view

23 Mrs. Barney Rubble

24 Some nest eggs, briefly

25 Bulletin board fastener

29 "Fourscore and seven years ___ ..."

ACROSS

1 Aussie greeting
5 Witch trials town
10 Spaghetti sauce brand
11 Rival of 10-Across
12 Actor Guinness or Baldwin
13 New ___ Eve
14 Traffic stoppers?
16 "Rope-a-dope" boxer
17 Farmyard enclosure
18 Sucker
21 Colorful family card game
23 Pane in a picture window
28 ___-ski
29 Flapjack franchise, briefly
30 Egg beater
31 Mouselike rodent
32 Mean-spirited
33 Examined

DOWN

1 Mortarboard tosser
2 Salvador who painted melting watches
3 "Rock of ___"
4 Desert plant with sword-shaped leaves
5 Network of secret agents
6 General vicinity
7 Jobs for plumbers
8 White marsh bird
9 Like some tree trunks
15 Feature of a cloudless day

18 Give rise to
19 First Greek letter
20 Louvre locale
22 Garnish for a
   martini
24 Experiment
25 Mariner's greeting
26 One and only
27 Risked getting a
   ticket

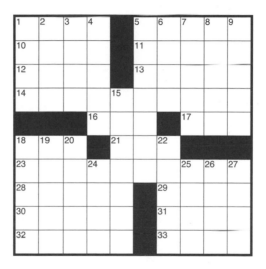

ACROSS

1 Home of Godzilla
6 Draped garment
10 Plain People of Pennsylvania
11 Burden
12 Area of traffic congestion
14 ___ terrier (Scottish dog breed)
15 Chop finely
16 Crater's edge
18 "Which way ___ they go?"
19 LaGuardia alternative, familiarly
22 Parting word
24 Lofty lair
26 Kennel comments
30 Watergate informant's pseudonym
32 Neighborhood kid in "Blondie"
33 Words after "Open up"
34 ___-in-the-wool
35 Little Bo Peep lost hers

DOWN

1 Pokes
2 Out of control
3 Feel sorry for
4 Autumn blossom
5 Stanley Cup org.
6 "The Bluest Eye" author Morrison
7 Without interruption
8 Big name in Italian fashion
9 Part of FAQ
13 Tube trophy
17 "A likely story!"

19 Bored with one's existence
20 Touchy-___
21 Word in several Dunkin' Donuts flavor names
23 Our world
25 Portable tune player
27 Kate's "Titanic" role
28 Partner of fortune
29 Dance move
31 That guy's

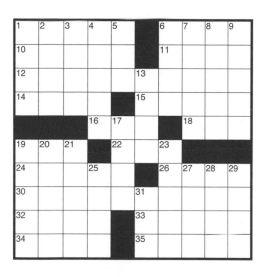

ACROSS
1 "See ya later"
6 Abbr. on a business envelope
10 Type of pipe
11 Twisted-apart treat
12 "Tastes great!" vs. "Less filling!" beer
14 Herbal ___
15 ___ populi
16 Knucklehead
19 "Lemon Tree" singer Lopez
21 Letter-shaped girders
23 American League division
24 "Wherefore ___ thou Romeo?"
25 Greek letter between chi and omega
27 Cable channel with classic sitcoms
32 Fruity soda brand
33 Frightfully strange
34 "Orinoco Flow" singer
35 Practical joke

DOWN
1 Company nicknamed "Big Blue"
2 Hospital scan, for short
3 Slick liquid
4 Hesitate
5 Priceless?
6 Instant messaging pioneer
7 "Jeopardy!" material
8 Mountain range near Yellowstone Park

9 "You can't get out this way" sign
13 Lab animal
16 Senator Feinstein
17 "Conan" host
18 Uneven in quality
20 Actor Carl or Rob
22 Place to unwind
26 "Watch your ___!"
28 South Korean car company
29 Roth ___ (savings plan)
30 Three-letter metal
31 Cry of mock fright

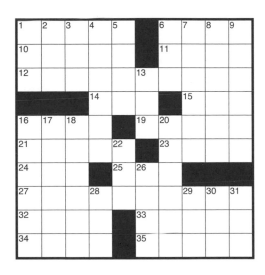

ACROSS

1 Omelet ingredients
5 PBS talk show host Smiley
10 Spot on the radar
11 Put into office
12 Old TV clown
13 Open courtyards
14 Explorer on the Red Planet
16 Suds dispenser
17 Before, in poetry
18 Sugary drink
21 "Chocolate" dog breed, briefly
23 Tennis racket area where optimal contact is made
27 Car rental chain
28 Hawaiian feast
30 Upper crust
31 Commando weapons
32 Take the wheel
33 Exclusive

DOWN

1 Subside
2 Grab (onto)
3 Great Pyramid locale
4 Plastic picnic utensil
5 Riot squad's supply
6 Female choir voice
7 Pizzazz
8 Less cordial
9 Long gaze
15 Effervescent beverage
18 Campfire leftovers
19 Inhabited
20 Causing goosebumps

22 Pretty good grade
24 Ending for major or novel
25 Greek liqueur
26 Manx cat's lack
29 "What's the ___?"

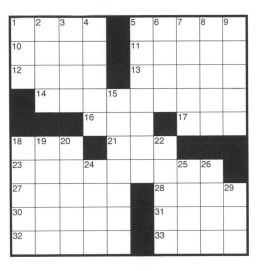

ACROSS

1 Sci-fi escape vehicles
5 "___ Rocks" (SeaWorld show)
10 In the ___ (informed)
11 Falcon's claw
12 Hall of Fame shortstop with 13 Gold Glove Awards
14 Tractor name
15 Garden pond fish
16 Belgian seaport
19 Fox hunter's cry
22 Gp. with a noted journal
23 Make into law
27 Kermit the Frog's joke-telling buddy
30 Unleashed
31 "___ la Douce"
32 Type of basic question
33 Gunky stuff

DOWN

1 Trudge along
2 Move like the Blob
3 Take a siesta
4 Staircase shape
5 They're numbered in NYC
6 "Green Eggs and ___"
7 Much the same
8 Part of DMV
9 Not part of the cool crowd
13 Start of a counting rhyme
17 Biblical pronoun
18 Struck it rich
19 Chewy, stretchy candy

20 Dean Martin's "That's ___"

21 Takes it easy

24 Flying start?

25 GI garb, at times

26 Device that's sprung

28 Branch of Buddhism

29 Chapel vow

1	2	3	4		5	6	7	8	9
10					11				
12				13					
14							15		
			16		17	18			
19	20	21							
22					23		24	25	26
27			28	29					
30						31			
32						33			

ACROSS

1 Stiff and sore
5 Hero of "The Lion King"
10 Fruit that flavors gin
11 Small hill
12 Sweet treat on a stick
14 Rush Limbaugh's medium
15 They're above abs
16 Authorizes
17 Dieter's concern
19 "Mad ___" (Mel Gibson movie)
20 "The Biggest Loser" network
23 Nodder's words
26 Send with a click
28 Sweet treat on a stick
30 Air Force One, for one
31 Made stuff up
32 Like a bubble bath
33 Country road

DOWN

1 Houston ballplayer
2 ___-and-dagger
3 Ruffians
4 Mythical Himalayan beast
5 Take to the slopes
6 Hardly handy
7 Act gloomy
8 Coalition
9 Mountains in "The Sound of Music"
13 Couch potato's place
18 Chopped down
19 Intends
20 Gymnast Comaneci

21 Name below
Obama on
bumper stickers
22 Bonnie's outlaw
partner
23 DSL offerers
24 "Star Trek"
helmsman
25 "My word!"
27 Sbarro locale,
often
29 Marina del ___,
California

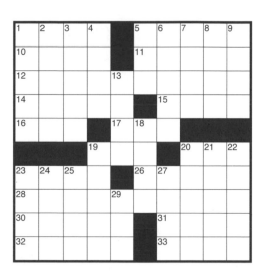

ACROSS

1 Go down the tubes
5 Italian motor scooter brand
10 Prefix for potent
11 Constellation with a belt
12 Reassuring response to "Are you hurt?"
13 Word on a triangular traffic sign
14 Hero who rode Silver, with "the"
16 Toto or Benji, e.g.
17 Palindromic preposition
18 "___ had it up to here!"
21 Actor DiCaprio, to fans
23 One who's left the band
28 Cover story
29 Light headwear?
30 Give a wide berth to
31 Subjects for Freud
32 Dove houses
33 Seating sections

DOWN

1 Shiny food wrapper
2 Firearm filler
3 A part of
4 Took a shine to
5 Traveler
6 "___ Brockovich"
7 Prolonged attack
8 Person propelling a gondola
9 Wrestling legend ___ the Giant
15 Antacid brand that "spells relief"

18 "I, Robot" author Asimov
19 Automaker headquartered in Sweden
20 "Silas Marner" author George
22 Survey category
24 New York theater award
25 Undoer of Othello
26 ___ news day
27 Soft throw

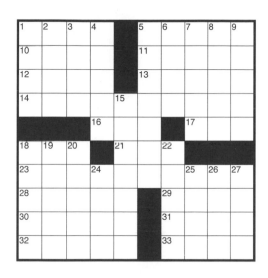

ACROSS

1 Herd animal of the Andes
6 Kunis of "Black Swan"
10 Washroom fixture
11 Going ___ (brawling)
12 Corn bread cooked on a griddle
14 "You don't say!"
15 "Glee" star ___ Michele
16 Combination lock feature
19 Works like a dog
21 Eyeballed rudely
23 Comical Martha
24 It's between Mon. and Wed.
25 NATO member
27 Capital of Nevada
32 No longer fooled by
33 Single-handedly
34 Sloop pole
35 Fellows

DOWN

1 '60s White House initials
2 ___-tzu (Chinese philosopher)
3 Volcanic fallout
4 Do some socializing at a party
5 "The Vampire Chronicles" author Rice
6 Big Apple product?
7 Roma's country
8 Quite possible
9 Boot camp command
13 Up to now

16 Web-based business
17 Tropical lizard
18 Heads-up notices
20 Source of ancient prophecies
22 Twosome
26 Pantyhose woe
28 Boozer
29 Particle with a charge
30 Blaster's letters
31 "May I help you?"

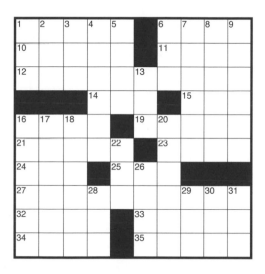

ACROSS

1 French painter of "Olympia"
6 Sulk
10 Powerful adhesive
11 "We try harder" company
12 Party hearty
13 Profound
14 Tennessee museum dedicated to Elvis Presley
16 Slalom skier's path
17 "Platoon" setting, briefly
18 North Atlantic catch
19 ___ Beta Kappa
22 Tennessee amusement park owned by country singer Parton
25 ___ boots ('60s footwear)
26 Pleasant, as weather
27 Poet Pound
28 Nerdy "Family Matters" character
29 Mild-mannered
30 Twist out of shape

DOWN

1 Become one
2 Simon Says players
3 Exploding stars
4 Biz hotshot
5 Headache remedy
6 Respectful address
7 Microwave, for example
8 ___ Piper
9 Mind reader's ability
15 Red-and-black aphid eater
18 Garb for a wizard

19 Oktoberfest dance
20 Regular at Moe's Tavern
21 Pastoral poem
22 Nod off
23 Storybook villain
24 Put on guard
25 Ruby or onyx

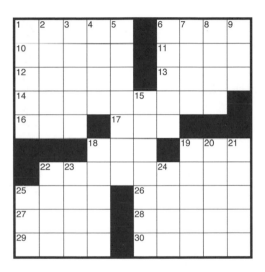

ACROSS

1 Ghastly
6 Amino ___
10 Thick-skinned herbivore
11 When summer starts
12 Class of international auto racing
14 Matching
15 Followed a curved path
16 Jerry's cartoon nemesis
18 Surgery sites, for short
19 No longer chic
22 Quayle and Biden, briefly
24 What Kix and Trix do
26 Corned beef dish
30 Football game played on January 15, 1967
32 Finds in mines
33 Kitchen garment
34 Zilch, in Zacatecas
35 Thus far

DOWN

1 Comical dog sounds
2 "Hold it right there!"
3 Law ___ (attorneys' workplace)
4 Not achieved, as goals
5 Hulk portrayer Ferrigno
6 Slightly open
7 Kaley of "The Big Bang Theory"
8 Word with city or circle
9 Monopoly cards
13 Aladdin's discovery

| 83

17 "___ my dead
   body!"
19 Welles of old
   Hollywood
20 "Star Trek"
   communications
   officer
21 Composed with a
   keyboard
23 Patronizes the
   mall
25 City in Arizona
27 Haywire
28 Plumlike fruit
29 Solving aid
31 Petting zoo bleat

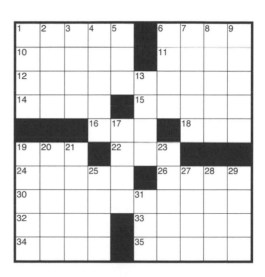

ACROSS

1 Speak boastfully
5 Movie, in slang
10 U2 frontman
11 Hawaiian island or patio
12 Champagne glass feature
13 "The Jetsons" dog
14 Nickname for the "Welcome Back, Kotter" students
16 Pimple
17 Moo goo gai pan pan

18 Hardwood tree
21 Baseball great Carew
23 Site of an ill-fated 1961 invasion
27 Cornhusker State city
28 "Saving Private ___"
30 Small engine
31 Chicago paper, familiarly
32 Scrub in the tub
33 Diminutive "Empire Strikes Back" guru

DOWN

1 Air rifle ammo
2 Decays
3 From square one
4 Father of Wednesday and Pugsley Addams
5 '50s haircut for men
6 Mascara spot
7 Being pulled along
8 Ship's load
9 Newsstand booth
15 Delta or American charge

18 Manhattan Project
    project, briefly
19 South Pacific
    island group
20 Marriott rival
22 Play ___ (cheat)
24 Eager student's cry
25 Greek deli order
26 Put into words
29 Where to find
    Mavs and Cavs

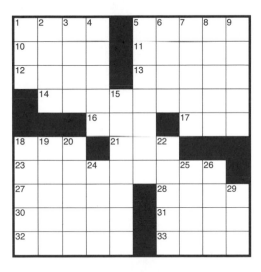

ACROSS

1 Leaves at the altar
6 High cards
10 Digital read
11 Ingrid's role in "Casablanca"
12 Frozen treat created using liquid nitrogen
14 Mental invention
15 Hall's singing partner
16 ___ code (envelope number)
18 "Yo!"
19 Surface for curling
22 Playboy mogul, familiarly
24 Nearsighted cartoon Mr.
26 Enlist again
30 Memorable moments
32 OPEC member
33 All-night dance parties
34 Barcelona bull
35 Chamber in a tomb

DOWN

1 Movie knight
2 Footnote abbr.
3 Run with long, easy strides
4 November birthstone
5 Enjoy Aspen
6 Verdi opera about a slave
7 Fabric
8 Cosmetician Lauder
9 Smart-mouthed
13 "Forget it!"
17 Breakfast chain acronym
19 "They shot me!"
20 Africa's largest city

21 Samantha of "The Collector"

23 Monastery resident

25 "This is a disaster!"

27 "Green-eyed" feeling

28 Coll. near the Mexican border

29 18-Across alternative

31 Monster in "The Lord of the Rings"

ACROSS

1 Roo's mom
6 Skirt borders
10 "I do" sayer
11 Water, to Javier
12 Fairy tale villain who huffs and puffs
14 Sch. in Baton Rouge
15 Land in la mer
16 Japan's highest mountain
19 Short-lived '50s Ford model
21 Correct, as text
23 DOJ employee
24 Vinyl records
25 James Bond, e.g.
27 Member of Robin Hood's Merry Men
32 Three-layer cookie
33 "M*A*S*H" setting
34 "What ___ you thinking?"
35 Black piano key material

DOWN

1 Cold War intelligence org.
2 Onassis nickname
3 Eggy drink
4 Creature akin to a gnome
5 Latin I word
6 "Hee ___"
7 Puffed-up person
8 Hairstyle that's short in the front and long in the back
9 With caution
13 Expected
16 Chap
17 Diamond authority
18 King's entertainer

20 "Don't quit your ___!"
22 Broadband choice, briefly
26 Chinese lap dog, for short
28 Tip of a shoe
29 "___ y plata" (motto of Montana)
30 Rooster's mate
31 Disapproving vote

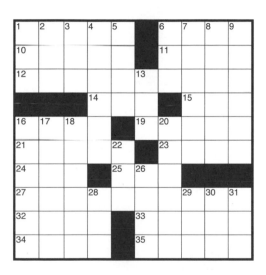

90

7
P	E	C	A	N		J	A	M	S
S	L	O	P	E		O	W	I	E
S	M	A	R	T	P	H	O	N	E
T	O	T	O		O	N	K	E	Y
		N	F	L		E	R	A	
E	L	F		L	E	E			
L	O	U	I	E		V	E	T	O
D	U	M	B	W	A	I	T	E	R
E	P	E	E		S	T	A	R	Z
R	E	S	T		P	A	T	I	O

9
R	A	M	S		L	A	M	A	S
A	T	O	P		E	X	A	C	T
N	A	P	E		A	L	L	E	Y
D	R	E	W	B	R	E	E	S	
B	I	D	S	O	N				
			M	E	T	H	O	D	
	S	E	A	B	R	E	E	Z	E
B	U	R	M	A		S	L	O	B
B	L	I	P	S		L	I	N	T
Q	U	E	S	T		A	X	E	S

11
M	E	A	T		E	B	S	E	N
G	Y	R	O		S	L	O	M	O
M	E	T	R	O	P	O	L	I	S
			M	O	N	T	A	N	A
S	W	E	E	P			C	E	L
P	I	A		K	R	E	M	E	
I	N	S	T	Y	L	E			
G	O	T	H	A	M	C	I	T	Y
O	N	E	A	M		A	R	E	A
T	A	R	T	S		P	E	A	K

13
F	O	R	D	S		O	U	T	S
U	B	O	A	T		P	H	E	W
T	O	W	N	S	Q	U	A	R	E
Z	E	S	T		U	S	U	R	P
		E	T	A		L	I	T	
W	E	S		A	Y	E			
I	N	T	E	L		L	A	K	E
C	R	O	P	C	I	R	C	L	E
C	O	U	P		M	O	T	E	L
A	N	T	S		O	Y	V	E	Y

15
T	A	S	K		W	H	E	A	T
O	D	I	E		P	E	P	P	Y
P	O	O	R		M	I	S	E	R
P	R	U	N	E		D	O	D	O
S	E	X		G	R	I	M		
		F	L	O	E		D	O	M
D	U	A	L		D	R	O	N	E
I	S	L	A	M		A	W	E	S
V	E	L	M	A		G	N	U	S
E	S	S	A	Y		E	S	P	Y

17
R	O	M	A		C	R	E	P	E
E	V	I	L		P	E	R	I	L
H	A	M	M	E	R	L	O	C	K
A	T	E	A	M		A	S	K	S
B	E	D		M	A	X			
			G	Y	M		P	A	L
A	C	T	I		M	A	R	I	O
N	A	I	L	P	O	L	I	S	H
T	I	L	D	E		B	E	L	A
I	N	L	A	W		A	D	E	N

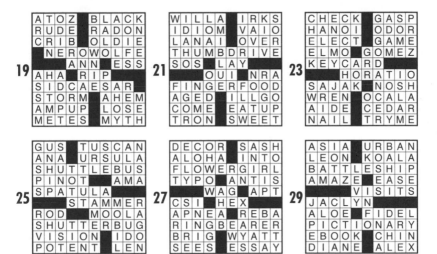

19

A	T	O	Z		B	L	A	C	K
R	U	D	E		R	A	D	O	N
C	R	I	B		O	L	D	I	E
	N	E	R	O	W	O	L	F	E
		A	N	N		E	S	S	
A	H	A		R	I	P			
S	I	D	C	A	E	S	A	R	
S	T	O	R	M		A	H	E	M
A	M	P	U	P		L	O	S	E
M	E	T	E	S		M	Y	T	H

21

W	I	L	L	A		I	R	K	S
I	D	I	O	M		V	A	I	O
L	A	N	A	I		O	V	E	R
T	H	U	M	B	D	R	I	V	E
S	O	S		L	A	Y			
		O	U	I		N	R	A	
F	I	N	G	E	R	F	O	O	D
A	G	E	D		I	L	L	G	O
C	O	M	E		E	A	T	U	P
T	R	O	N		S	W	E	E	T

23

C	H	E	C	K		G	A	S	P
H	A	N	O	I		O	D	O	R
E	L	E	C	T		G	A	M	E
E	L	M	O		G	O	M	E	Z
K	E	Y	C	A	R	D			
			H	O	R	A	T	I	O
S	A	J	A	K		N	O	S	H
W	R	E	N		O	C	A	L	A
A	I	D	E		C	E	D	A	R
N	A	I	L		T	R	Y	M	E

25

G	U	S		T	U	S	C	A	N
A	N	A		U	R	S	U	L	A
S	H	U	T	T	L	E	B	U	S
P	I	N	O	T		A	M	A	
S	P	A	T	U	L	A			
			S	T	A	M	M	E	R
R	O	D		M	O	O	L	A	
S	H	U	T	T	E	R	B	U	G
V	I	S	I	O	N		I	D	O
P	O	T	E	N	T		L	E	N

27

D	E	C	O	R		S	A	S	H
A	L	O	H	A		I	N	T	O
F	L	O	W	E	R	G	I	R	L
T	Y	P	O		A	N	T	I	S
			W	A	G		A	P	T
C	S	I		H	E	X			
A	P	N	E	A		R	E	B	A
R	I	N	G	B	E	A	R	E	R
B	R	I	G		W	Y	A	T	T
S	E	E	S		E	S	S	A	Y

29

A	S	I	A		U	R	B	A	N
L	E	O	N		K	O	A	L	A
B	A	T	T	L	E	S	H	I	P
A	M	A	Z	E		E	A	S	E
			V	I	S	I	T	S	
J	A	C	L	Y	N				
A	L	O	E		F	I	D	E	L
P	I	C	T	I	O	N	A	R	Y
E	B	O	O	K		C	H	I	N
D	I	A	N	E		A	L	E	X

31

C	A	T	E		L	O	B	E	S
H	E	W	N		A	A	R	O	N
A	R	I	D		R	H	I	N	O
P	I	X	I	E	C	U	T		
S	E	T	T	L	E				
			I	N	V	A	D	E	
	P	I	X	Y	S	T	I	X	
H	E	I	D	I		I	S	N	T
A	M	B	E	R		G	E	E	R
T	U	B	A	S		N	A	D	A

33

A	N	G	L	E		F	I	J	I
W	U	R	S	T		I	R	I	S
F	R	E	D	S	A	V	A	G	E
U	S	E			D	E	N	S	E
L	E	N	S	C	A	P			
			H	A	M	M	O	C	K
A	V	I	A	N			D	R	E
S	I	D	V	I	C	I	O	U	S
K	N	E	E		A	M	U	S	E
S	E	A	R		F	O	R	T	Y

35

T	U	F	T	S		S	O	L	E
C	H	E	E	K		A	V	I	D
B	A	R	N	E	Y	F	I	F	E
Y	U	M		L	E	A	D	E	N
		L	I	N	E	A	R		
			E	T	H	I	C	S	
S	E	A	W	A	Y		A	L	A
K	E	T	T	L	E	D	R	U	M
I	N	T	O		A	D	O	R	E
D	Y	A	N		H	E	L	P	S

37

S	M	U	R	F		H	E	R	A
K	O	R	E	A		O	L	I	N
I	N	N	E	R	C	H	I	L	D
M	O	S	S		Z	O	O	E	Y
			E	P	A		T	D	S
P	A	T		U	R	L			
I	C	I	E	R		A	L	A	S
O	U	T	E	R	S	P	A	C	E
U	R	A	L		E	S	S	E	X
S	A	N	S		W	E	E	D	Y

39

B	O	R	N		O	L	M	O	S
O	B	E	Y		B	E	A	U	T
D	O	N	Q	U	I	X	O	T	E
S	E	O	U	L			R	T	E
			I	N	I	T	I	A	L
D	E	C	L	A	R	E			
I	M	O		A	N	K	L	E	
D	A	I	R	Y	Q	U	E	E	N
S	I	N	A	I		R	E	A	D
O	L	S	E	N		E	L	K	S

41

G	A	P	S		A	C	C	R	A
A	V	O	W		R	A	R	E	R
B	R	E	A	D	F	R	U	I	T
L	I	M	B	O		O	D	D	S
E	L	S		J	A	M			
			M	O	M		A	H	A
O	B	O	E		O	A	T	E	N
B	U	T	T	E	R	B	E	A	N
I	N	T	E	L		C	A	V	E
S	T	O	R	K		S	T	Y	X

92

43

P	A	L	S		P	A	B	S	T
A	B	E	T		A	L	L	I	E
T	O	G	A		R	O	U	S	T
H	U	G	H	L	A	U	R	I	E
S	T	Y	L	E	S				
				A	O	R	T	A	S
P	E	T	E	R	L	O	R	R	E
O	C	E	A	N		D	I	R	E
S	H	A	V	E		I	P	O	D
H	O	S	E	D		N	E	W	S

45

A	D	L	I	B		P	A	G	E
P	E	O	N	Y		A	L	A	S
E	A	G	L	E	S	C	O	U	T
S	L	O	E		E	T	U	D	E
			T	E	X		D	Y	E
J	I	M		A	Y	E			
U	M	A	S	S		V	E	E	R
M	E	R	I	T	B	A	D	G	E
P	A	I	N		I	D	E	A	L
S	N	A	G		B	E	N	D	Y

47

G	A	R	B	O		N	O	U	N
O	D	O	R	S		Y	U	R	I
D	O	U	B	L	E	M	I	N	T
I	N	G			O	O	P		
V	I	E	W		S	H	R	E	K
A	S	S	E	T		S	O	L	O
			B	O	A		T	O	T
J	U	I	C	Y	F	R	U	I	T
O	K	R	A		R	I	N	S	E
T	E	E	M		O	D	D	E	R

49

F	I	Z	Z	Y		A	M	F	M
A	D	I	E	U		N	A	L	A
W	E	T	B	L	A	N	K	E	T
N	A	I	R		G	E	E	S	E
			A	B	E		S	H	Y
U	M	P		U	S	C			
N	A	R	C	S		O	D	E	S
C	R	A	Z	Y	Q	U	I	L	T
A	I	D	A		B	R	O	M	O
P	O	O	R		S	T	R	O	P

51

S	P	A	S	M		T	H	A	W
A	L	I	T	O		V	E	R	A
G	E	S	U	N	D	H	E	I	T
S	A	L		G	O	O	D	A	T
	D	E	F	O	G	S			
			R	O	T	T	E	N	
A	S	S	I	S	I		X	I	I
W	U	N	D	E	R	K	I	N	D
E	L	I	A		E	A	S	E	L
D	U	T	Y		D	I	T	S	Y

53

P	E	P	S	I		P	R	I	M
A	D	L	I	B		L	E	N	O
T	W	I	L	L		U	N	D	O
T	I	N	K	E	R	T	O	Y	S
I	N	K		W	O	O			
			J	I	B		A	S	S
E	R	E	C	T	O	R	S	E	T
G	E	A	R		C	O	W	E	R
G	A	V	E		O	S	A	K	A
S	P	E	W		P	A	N	S	Y

55

```
A B B A   L I N D A
T E A S   O N I O N
B A T H T U B G I N
A D I E U   O H N O
T S K   B M X
      B A Y   J A N
A J A R   T H E R E
B A B Y S H O W E R
E D U C E   P E N D
L A T E X   S L A Y
```

57

```
S C A R   B I R D S
A U R A   U R I A H
S K I N   G O N Z O
H E A D B A N G E R
    B U B   O D E
E B B   L O U
F O O T L O C K E R
L I T U P   O N C E
A S O N E   N E H I
T E X A N   N E O N
```

59

```
P A L M   B L A B S
T I E R   A I M A T
A L O H A S T A T E
    Y A K   N B A
A S A D A   I D O L
R O P E   B D A Y S
C R O   L E I
H E L L O D O L L Y
I S L E T   C I A O
E T O N S   Y U G O
```

61

```
A N T O N   S T E P
N E R D Y   H A L O
V A U D E V I L L E
I T S   O N E A M
L O S E S I T
    M A D O N N A
A L I B I   A I R
V I R A L V I D E O
O M A R   A S I C S
W O N K   T H R E E
```

63

```
C E S A R   S W A B
A L I V E   N A S A
R I L E D   A C H E
P O L   W O R K E R
S T Y   I N K Y
    P A N E   R O B
I T U N E S   A P E
R A T T   T A C I T
A C T S   A G E N T
S K Y Y   R O S E Y
```

65

```
G D A Y   S A L E M
R A G U   P R E G O
A L E C   Y E A R S
D I S C B R A K E S
    A L I   S T Y
S A P   U N O
P L A T E G L A S S
A P R E S   I H O P
W H I S K   V O L E
N A S T Y   E Y E D
```

67

J	A	P	A	N		T	O	G	A
A	M	I	S	H		O	N	U	S
B	O	T	T	L	E	N	E	C	K
S	K	Y	E		M	I	N	C	E
			R	I	M		D	I	D
J	F	K		B	Y	E			
A	E	R	I	E		A	R	F	S
D	E	E	P	T	H	R	O	A	T
E	L	M	O		I	T	S	M	E
D	Y	E	D		S	H	E	E	P

69

I	M	O	F	F		A	T	T	N
B	R	I	A	R		O	R	E	O
M	I	L	L	E	R	L	I	T	E
			T	E	A		V	O	X
D	O	P	E		T	R	I	N	I
I	B	A	R	S		E	A	S	T
A	R	T		P	S	I			
N	I	C	K	A	T	N	I	T	E
N	E	H	I		E	E	R	I	E
E	N	Y	A		P	R	A	N	K

71

E	G	G	S		T	A	V	I	S
B	L	I	P		E	L	E	C	T
B	O	Z	O		A	T	R	I	A
	M	A	R	S	R	O	V	E	R
			K	E	G		E	R	E
A	D	E		L	A	B			
S	W	E	E	T	S	P	O	T	
H	E	R	T	Z		L	U	A	U
E	L	I	T	E		U	Z	I	S
S	T	E	E	R		S	O	L	E

95

73

P	O	D	S		S	H	A	M	U
L	O	O	P		T	A	L	O	N
O	Z	Z	I	E	S	M	I	T	H
D	E	E	R	E		K	O	I	
			A	N	T	W	E	R	P
T	A	L	L	Y	H	O			
A	M	A			E	N	A	C	T
F	O	Z	Z	I	E	B	E	A	R
F	R	E	E	D		I	R	M	A
Y	E	S	N	O		G	O	O	P

75

A	C	H	Y		S	I	M	B	A
S	L	O	E		K	N	O	L	L
T	O	O	T	S	I	E	P	O	P
R	A	D	I	O		P	E	C	S
O	K	S		F	A	T			
			M	A	X		N	B	C
I	S	E	E		E	M	A	I	L
S	U	G	A	R	D	A	D	D	Y
P	L	A	N	E		L	I	E	D
S	U	D	S	Y		L	A	N	E

77

F	A	I	L		V	E	S	P	A
O	M	N	I		O	R	I	O	N
I	M	O	K		Y	I	E	L	D
L	O	N	E	R	A	N	G	E	R
			D	O	G		E	R	E
I	V	E		L	E	O			
S	O	L	O	A	R	T	I	S	T
A	L	I	B	I		H	A	L	O
A	V	O	I	D		E	G	O	S
C	O	T	E	S		R	O	W	S

79

```
LLAMA MILA
BASIN ATIT
JOHNNYCAKE
   GEE LEA
DIAL TOILS
OGLED RAYE
TUE USA
CARSONCITY
ONTO ALONE
MAST GENTS
```

81

```
MANET MOPE
EPOXY AVIS
REVEL DEEP
GRACELAND
ESS NAM
   COD PHI
 DOLLYWOOD
GOGO BALMY
EZRA URKEL
MEEK GNARL
```

83

```
AWFUL ACID
RHINO JUNE
FORMULAONE
SAME ARCED
   TOM ORS
OUT VPS
RHYME HASH
SUPERBOWLI
ORES APRON
NADA ASYET
```

85

```
BRAG FLICK
BONO LANAI
STEM ASTRO
 SWEATHOGS
  ZIT WOK
ASH ROD
BAYOFPIGS
OMAHA RYAN
MOTOR TRIB
BATHE YODA
```

87

```
JILTS ACES
EBOOK ILSA
DIPPINDOTS
IDEA OATES
  ZIP HEY
ICE HEF
MAGOO REUP
HIGHPOINTS
IRAN RAVES
TORO CRYPT
```

89

```
KANGA HEMS
GROOM AGUA
BIGBADWOLF
   LSU ILE
FUJI EDSEL
EMEND ATTY
LPS SPY
LITTLEJOHN
OREO KOREA
WERE EBONY
```

96